NEURO PRIMING FOR PEAK PERFORMANCE

Customizing Tennis Audio Recordings

By

Frank Giampaolo

Copyright 2017

Also Available By Frank Giampaolo

Championship Tennis
(Human Kinetics Worldwide Publishing)

The Tennis Parent's Bible 2nd Edition

Emotional Aptitude In Sports
Stop Choking In Competition

Raising Athletic Royalty:
Insights to Inspire for a Lifetime

International Player Evaluation

The Mental Emotional Tennis Work Books Series:
Blunders and Cures
Match Chart Collection
Match Day Preparation
How to Attract a College Scholarship

Website:
http://www.MaximizingTennisPotential.com

Printed by Createspace

COVER PHOTO: **Katie LaFrance**

DEDICATION

This book is dedicated to my amazing stepdaughter Sarah Isabel Fansler. Sarah started her tennis career at age 10. She competed at the US Open by the age of 15. She is living proof that an athlete can reach world-class status in 5000 hours if a dedicated, customized developmental plan is in place.

FOREWORD

By Steve Johnson, ATP Tennis Professional

As a professional ATP tennis player, I know all too well the importance of positive mental imagery as it relates to playing at my peak performance level.

Neuro Priming for Peak Performance is an innovative instructional book that takes the mystery out of the visualization process. It organizes mental rehearsals into customized scripts designed to improve every component of a tennis player's game.

I've been friends with Frank since I was a junior player. His outside the box approach to organizing and training mental and emotional skill sets is groundbreaking. Frank's *Neuro Priming* workbook motivates athletes to stop focusing on what could go wrong and instead, start focusing on what can go right. It's the laws of attraction - the psychology of success.

Neuro Priming for Peak Performance is an indispensable tool for every serious-minded tennis competitor, parent or coach.

CONTENTS

ACKNOWLEDGMENT

This short list of tennis industry friends inspirit great leadership qualities and inspire me daily: Shaul Zohar, Johan Kriek, Tim Mayotte, Craig Tiley, Jenny Walls Robb, Jim Harp, Lane Evans, Alvin Cheng, Bill Riddle, Chuck Gill, Andy Dowsett, Alec Horton, Steve Tier, Ken DeHart, Wes Fuller, Steve Johnson Sr., Craig Bell, Styrling Strother, Julio Godreau, Craig O'Shannessy, Lisa Goodman Stone, Allistar McCaw, Michelle Krause, Joel Drucker, Jim Harp, Brian Parkkonen, Larry Scalia, Sarah Jane Stone, Hassan Humayun, Emma Doyle, Adrin Himmelheber, Dave Borelli, Dan Beedle, Susan Nardi, Bill Patton, Julie Jilly, Nick Weatley, Mary Pat Faley, Mark Kovacs, PJ Simmons, Colin Foster, Dick Gould, Peter Smith, Adam Blicher, Fiesal Hassan, Jorge Capestany, Neil Biddle, Jeff Salzenstein, Angel Lopez, Trever Kronemane, Craig Cignarrelli, and Desmond Oon. Innovation is essential and these folks encourage and influence me constantly.

INTRODUCTION

In the medical field, heart surgeons report that if they practiced the way they did just five years ago, they would have been sued for malpractice. Yet, in the business of coaching tennis, teaching professionals all too often teach the same fundamental systems they were taught decades ago. Dedicating most tennis training to grooving forehands and backhands and neglecting training what's between the ears. Success in the competitive game of tennis is dependent on emotional and mental warfare.

I've found that only training an athlete's hardware (stroke fundamentals & athleticism) and ignoring their software (mental and emotional), often results in match-day disappointment due to underdeveloped competitive skills.

Researchers estimated that even with the best teachers, students typically walk away from their training sessions retaining approximately 20% of the coach's advice. So to help reinforce lesson instruction, I recommend applying customized neuro priming.

Neuro priming involves mental imagery to review and rehearse solutions for competitive performance. This visualization process is an essential off-court form of training personalized to each athlete with advanced solutions designed for specific match play situations. Neuroscientists report that athletes who apply personalized mental rehearsals drastically improve performance during match play. I consider neuro priming not only fundamental for competitive athletes but often the missing link for athletes unable to compete under stress at their full potential.

"Competitive successes or failures aren't the results of a singular performance, but the result of the athlete's physical, mental and emotional routines and rituals."

This guidebook provides a fresh, unique pathway to improving tennis skills with a customized script, in the athlete's very own voice via a series of audio recordings on their phone. Neural priming is not meant to replace an athlete's on-court tennis training. It is an essential enhancement of their mental, emotional and physical skills. Just as priming muscles before competition increases athleticism, neuro priming increases cognitive processing speed.

The Benefits of *Neuro Priming For Peak Performance* Includes:

- Increased confidence
- Enhanced match awareness
- Quickened cognitive processing speed
- Improved the mind-body neuro connection
- Greater tactical awareness
- Stroke flaw awareness & solutions
- Conflict resolution
- Stress management
- Opponent awareness
- Score management
- Choking & panicking resolution
- Problem-solving skills
- Enhanced strategic responses
- Improved emotional responses
- Staying on script (patterns and plays)

- Decreased worry, stress and fear
- Advanced resiliency
- Increased motivation
- Less hesitation
- Increased developmental organization
- Upgraded focus ability
- Enhanced concentration

The Sports Science of Neuro Priming

Neuroscientists report that mental rehearsal activates a network of neural coded motor programs in the brain that when primed activate the athlete's correct physiological responses. By creating customized audio recordings and then routinely listening to the recordings, the athlete strengthens the neural pathways required for competition.

Why Neuro Priming Works

Mental rehearsal is a form of preventative medicine. It identifies the causes of an athlete's anxiety. Neuro priming pin-points the possible problems and pre-sets their solutions. Performing at peak performance level requires the athlete to be confident and able to adapt when things go astray. In competitive matches, the athlete who has their pre-set contingency plans has superior confidence in their problem-solving ability.

Neuro priming is one of an athlete's greatest defenses against performance anxieties. It assists the athlete in trading in pessimism for optimism. (Note: Neuro priming may be a 3 - second between-point visualization routine or up to a 20-minute complete pre-competition review.)

ATP and WTA touring professionals are often quoted as saying the game is 90% mental and 10% physical. Neuro priming is a cutting-edge method to improve the mental and emotional components of a competitive athlete's tennis game. As I stated at the beginning, an athlete's routines and rituals ultimately define their success. I hope you find **Neuro Priming for Peak Performance** the key to maximizing your athlete's potential.

Designing and Recording Protocols

Neuro Priming for Peak Performance is organized into five chapters. Each chapter is devoted to a distinct tennis skill set. Designing an athlete's personalized audio recordings is best completed with a high EQ (Emotional Quota) coach or tennis mind. The following is a step by step for guide all five sections. *(Sample solutions for all five sections provided in Sample Solutions section beginning on page 59.)*

Step 1

With your coach, discuss each of the audio recording topics and complete your personalized script of solutions. These solutions should result from on-court training and most proficient patterns and tactics. The athlete should be able to perform the solutions routinely.

Step 2

Once solutions are identified, find a quiet space, eliminate all distractions, and get comfortable while you read your customized scripts into your cell phone's digital recorder. Allow 5 seconds in-between tips to enable time for adequate mental rehearsal visualization.

Step 3

Begin your mental rehearsals in a calm mental state by breathing deeply, eliminating muscle tension and controlling your wandering mind. While visualizing your physical, mental and emotional skill sets, apply realistic imagery using slow motion and real-time visualization.

Key Times for Neuro Priming

- Nightly before falling asleep, especially before matches.
- Early morning, when you're just waking up.
- Drive time/travel time.
- Before competitive matches.
- Between points & change-overs.
- After competition as a performance review.

AUDIO #1: Protocols for Stroke Production

For each primary and secondary stroke situation, write a short solution based catchphrase as a customized reminder. Athletes report that by mentally rehearsing their customized stroke solutions they not only fix their technical strokes quicker, they significantly reduce producing the actual errors. *(Sample Solutions: page 59)*

1) Forehands

Drive:

_____

_____

_____

_____

Short Angle:

_____

_____

_____

_____

High & Heavy:

_____

_____

_____

_____

Slice:

_____
_____
_____
_____

Drop Shot:

_____
_____
_____
_____

Lob:

_____
_____
_____
_____

2) Backhands

Drive:

_____
_____
_____
_____

Short Angle:

_____

_____

_____

_____

High & Heavy:

_____

_____

_____

_____

Slice:

_____

_____

_____

_____

Drop Shot:

_____

_____

_____

_____

Lob:

_____

_____

_____

_____

3) Serves

Flat:

_____
_____
_____
_____

Kick:

_____
_____
_____
_____

Slice:

_____
_____
_____
_____

4) Volleys

Punch:

_____
_____
_____
_____

Transition:

_____

_____

_____

_____

Swing:

_____

_____

_____

_____

Drop:

_____

_____

_____

_____

Half:

_____

_____

_____

_____

5) Specialty Lobs

Backing Up/ Topspin Lob:

_____

_____

_____

_____

Moving Forward/Slice Lob:

_____

_____

_____

_____

Re-Lob:

_____

_____

_____

_____

6) Approach Shot Sequence

Serve and Volley:

_____

_____

_____

_____

Chip & Charge:

_____

_____

_____

_____

Forehand Drive Approach:

_____

_____

_____

_____

Backhand Drive Approach:

_____

_____

_____

_____

Backhand Chip Approach:

_____

_____

_____

_____

High and Heavy Delayed Approach:

_____

_____

_____

_____

7) Overheads

Stationary:

_____

_____

_____

_____

Turn & Run:

_____

_____

_____

_____

AUDIO #2: Emotional Protocols

Design and list customized solutions for each of the emotional protocols. Athletes who mentally rehearse their pre-set contingency plans (emotional protocols) report cleaner performances and less match time drama consistently. *(Sample Solutions: page 62)*

My Between Point Rituals

External:

1) _____
_____
_____
_____

2) _____
_____
_____
_____

3) _____
_____
_____
_____

Internal:

1) _____
_____
_____
_____

2) _____
   _____
   _____
   _____

3) _____
   _____
   _____
   _____

My Changeover Rituals

External:

_____
_____
_____
_____

Internal:

_____
_____
_____
_____

Critical Times to Manage my Adrenaline

1) _____
   _____
   _____
   _____

2) _____
   _____
   _____
   _____

My Verbal & Physical Triggers to Combat Choking

Verbal:

_____
_____
_____
_____

Physical:

_____
_____
_____
_____

My Verbal & Physical Triggers for Panicking

Verbal:

_____
_____
_____
_____

Physical:

_____

_____

_____

_____

Energy Flow Management *(Check Box If Understood)*

☐ I'll control the playing speed of the match.

☐ I'll control the positive energy of the match.

☐ I'll inflate my fight to deflate their will to battle.

Game Day/Pre-Match Preparation
(Check Box If Understood)

☐ I will listen to my audio tapes to pre-set an excellent performance.

☐ I will morph into an athletic warrior by:

_____

_____

☐ I will warm up my primary & secondary strokes.

☐ I will go for a short run right before the match.

☐ I will focus on performing excellently ... not perfect.

☐ I will trust my training and my awesomeness.

Weekly Training Reminders *(Check Box If Understood)*

☐ I will record and watch my actual matches with a high IQ coach.

☐ I will focus my training on serving and returning serve.

☐ I will rehearse my top seven patterns weekly.

☐ I will pay attention to the cause of my errors.

☐ I will abide by "The Laws of Offense Neutral and Defensive" in my shots selections.

Letting Go of Perfectionism: *(Check Box If Understood)*

☐ I'll shoot for excellence, not perfection.

☐ I'll try to win 66% of the points.

☐ I'll relax and give 80% versus 110% effort.

☐ I'll eliminate energy-wasting antics.

AUDIO #3: Mental Protocols (SINGLES) Essentials

Design and list your customized strategic approach to the game of singles. Mentally rehearsing your solutions to the wide range of mental skills is fundamental in high-performance tennis. Athletes report that by customizing their mental solutions, they perform on script more consistently and efficiently. (*Sample Solutions: page 66*)

My "A" Game Plan Is:

_____

_____

_____

_____

My "B" Game Plan Is:

_____

_____

_____

_____

My shot tolerance level is_____

My Primary Top Seven Patterns

1) Most Proficient Pattern Serving to the Deuce Side:

_____

_____

_____

_____

2) Most Proficient Pattern Serving to the Advantage Side:

_____

_____

_____

_____

3) Most Proficient Return of Serve Position and Type of Return Versus a Big First Serve:

_____

_____

_____

_____

4) Most Proficient Return of Serve Position and Type of Return Versus a Weak or Second Serve:

_____

_____

_____

_____

5) Most Proficient Rally Pattern to Get Opponents Vulnerable:

_____

_____

_____

_____

6) Most Proficient Short Ball Options:

_____

_____

_____

_____

7) Most Proficient Net Rushing Patterns:

_____

_____

_____

_____

I Will Profile My Opponent's Game By
(Check box if understood)

- ☐ Recognize their "style" of play.
- ☐ Spot their favorite "top seven patterns" and shutting them down.
- ☐ Identify their "frustration tolerance" level.
- ☐ Determine their stroke and movement strengths and weaknesses.
- ☐ Recognize their "shot tolerance."

Score Management

Positive game points require:

_____

_____

_____

_____

Negative game points require:

_____

_____

_____

_____

Zonal Tennis

Court Zone Percentages:

_____

_____

_____

_____

Air Zone Percentages:

_____

_____

_____

_____

Broad Vision/Anticipatory Clues

_____

_____

_____

_____

Margins

I'll apply Safe Margins by:

_____
_____
_____
_____

Controlling the Baseline

1) I'll choose to hit forehands _____% of the time.

2) I'll choose to hit backhands _____% of the time.

Approaching the Net Wisely

1) I'll divide the width of the court into two zones.

2) I hit short balls landing in 75% of the court to their backhand and 25% to their forehand.

Two Tactical Changes to Consider When I'm Losing

1) Raising my level - hit harder, closer to the lines and attack successfully.

2) Sabotage their level - moonball, drop, slice, or junk ball.

Self-Destruction Solutions

1) If I'm losing to a "toad," I'll: *(Check Box If Understood)*

   ☐ Simply hit 3 balls down the center.
   ☐ Apply the "bounce-hit" method.
   ☐ Return to my script.
   ☐ Focus on simply winning 3 points in a row.

2) If my game isn't working and I'm losing to a retriever, I will pull them out of their comfort zone by:

   A) _____
   _____
   _____
   _____

   B) _____
   _____
   _____
   _____

   C) _____
   _____
   _____
   _____

3) If my game isn't working and I'm losing to a hard hitting baseliner, I will pull them out of their comfort zone by:

A) _____

_____

_____

_____

B) _____

_____

_____

_____

C) _____

_____

_____

_____

When to Choose Building Shots Versus Winners
(Check Box If Understood)

☐ Returning the first serve
☐ Rallying a deep ball
☐ On a negative mega point

AUDIO #4: Mental Protocols (DOUBLES) Essentials

Design and list your customized approach to the game of doubles by mentally rehearsing strategic solutions to the wide range of mental skills needed in high-performance tennis. Recognize that athletes report that by applying mental rehearsals, they prime the pumps and consistently perform better in competition. *(Sample Solutions: page 72)*

Choosing the Right Partner

A) Pick someone better than you. Name a few candidates:

_____

_____

_____

_____

B) The hammer & wedge partnership. Name a few candidates:

_____

_____

_____

_____

Warm Up For Doubles Matches with Doubles Skills Sets Not Singles *(Practice in the manner you're expected to perform):*

List 5 Warm-Up Doubles Strategies:

1) _____

_____

_____

_____

2) _____

_____

_____

_____

3) _____

_____

_____

_____

_____

4) _____

_____

_____

_____

5) _____

_____

_____

_____

Choosing Sides Deuce or Advantage Points to Consider:
(Check Box If Understood)

☐ Stroke strengths & weaknesses

☐ Emotional strengths & weaknesses

Partnership Communication

A) De-Stressing Topics (List 2)

1. _____

_____

_____

_____

2. _____
   _____
   _____
   _____

B) Opponent Profiling (List 2)

   1. _____
      _____
      _____
      _____

   2. _____
      _____
      _____
      _____

C) Tactical Options (List 2)

   1. _____
      _____
      _____
      _____

   2. _____
      _____
      _____
      _____

D) Facial Expressions, Body Language & Tone of Voice
   Matter (List 2)

   1. _____
      _____
      _____
      _____

2. _____
_____
_____
_____

E) Hand Signals Yes or No (List Signal)

_____
_____
_____
_____

Choose Your Best & 2nd Best Doubles System
(When & Why):

A) One Up and One Back

When:

_____
_____
_____
_____

Why:

_____
_____
_____
_____

B) Both Rush the Net

When:

_____
_____
_____
_____

Why:

_____

_____

_____

_____

C) Double Back

When:

_____

_____

_____

_____

Why:

_____

_____

_____

_____

D) "I" Formation

When:

_____

_____

_____

_____

Why:

_____

_____

_____

_____

The Role of Each Position in Doubles

A) Server:

_____

_____

_____

_____

B) Server's Partner:

_____

_____

_____

_____

C) Returner:

_____

_____

_____

_____

D) Returner's Partner:

_____

_____

_____

_____

Doubles Reminders *(Check Box If Understood)*

☐ Hit Long to long, short to short.

☐ Angles creates angles.

☐ Abide by the laws of offense, neutral and defense.

- [ ] High volleys are power volleys and low volleys are drop volleys.

- [ ] Net players have priority for any ball.

- [ ] When in doubt "Down the middle, solves the riddle."

- [ ] 70% of the points last 0-4 strikes, 20% last 5-9 and 10% go 10 & over.

- [ ] 78% of their winners come from their forehand and 22% from their backhand.

- [ ] Move together -synchronized with an imaginary 10 ft. ropes.

- [ ] Guard the center. (Only worry about your alley if your partner hits wide into the opposing doubles alley)

When to Poach

A.) Partner serves to the opponent's backhand.

_____

_____

_____

_____

B) Return of serve partner hits at the feet of the rushing server.

_____

_____

_____

_____

C.) Opponent is hitting inside strokes:

_____
_____
_____
_____

D.) Partner has hit "High and Heavy" & opponent is falling backward:

_____
_____
_____
_____

When to Choose a Building Shot Versus Going for a Risky Winner *(Check Box If Understood)*

□   Returning a solid first serve

□   Rallying a deep groundstroke

□   On a negative game point

Why Doubles is a Blast *(Check Box If Understood)*

☐ Less stressful because I'm sharing the fight.

☐ Teamwork in solving the physical, mental & emotional puzzles.

☐ My secondary strokes will improve.

☐ My problem-solving skills will improve.

☐ I'll get a great workout and warm up for singles.

AUDIO #5: Essential Life Skills Development

Upon the completion of the life skills assessment, any life skill graded a 7 or lower needs improvement. Google or YouTube, the definition of the life skill, then draft a paragraph describing your customized developmental plan to improve the skill. *(Sample Solutions: page 78)*

Life Skills Assessment

Increase your emotional aptitude by improving the following life skills. For each of the following life skills, grade your level of competence 1 through 10. (The number "1" represents an extreme weakness, and the number "10" represents an extreme strength.) Simply circle the number that best describes your comfort level.

Time Management: 1 2 3 4 5 6 7 8 9 10

The time management life skill is the ability to use one's time effectively or productively. A successful athlete with strong time management skills would organize daily, weekly, and monthly planners. Scheduling the development of each of the four major components (technical, athletic, mental, and emotional) essential to compete at the higher levels.

Adaptability: 1 2 3 4 5 6 7 8 9 10

The adaptability life skill is being able to adjust to different situations and conditions comfortably. To get the most from your physical talent, one must be open to change. Adapting is emotional intelligence at work.

Handling Adversity: 1 2 3 4 5 6 7 8 9 10

Handling adversity is a critical athletic and life skill. Competition brings hardship, drama, and suffering along with the positive attributes. Overcoming daily problems is a driving force of champions. Seeing adversity as a challenge versus a life or death crisis is key.

Handling Stress: 1 2 3 4 5 6 7 8 9 10

Stress causes biological and mental tension. It occurs when one believes that their physical skills aren't strong enough to meet the challenge. While some personalities stress more than others, proper preparation and a positive attitude dramatically reduce stress levels.

Perseverance: 1 2 3 4 5 6 7 8 9 10

Perseverance is one's ability to stay on course through setbacks, discouragement, injuries, and losses. It is the ability to fight stubbornly to achieve greatness.

Courage: 1 2 3 4 5 6 7 8 9 10

Courage is the ability to apply belief in your skills in spite of the threat at hand. Of course, if you aren't training at 100%, true courage doesn't exist. Courage is knowing that competition in sports is to be embraced and not feared. Courage is not allowing yourself to listen to the typical noise of "What if I lose."

Work Ethic: 1 2 3 4 5 6 7 8 9 10

Work ethic is a diligent, consistent standard of conduct. Strengthening physical, mental and emotional components and the attainment of goals is dependent on a deliberate customized plan and hard work.

Resiliency: 1 2 3 4 5 6 7 8 9 10

Resiliency is the capacity to recover and adjust after difficulties. Champions fall, hurt and fail just like us, but they have preset protocols to adapt and press on. Winners aren't always the most intelligent or even the strongest athletes in the event. They are often the individuals who respond with the best adjustments after misfortunes.

Goal Setting: 1 2 3 4 5 6 7 8 9 10

Goal setting is the process of identifying something that you want to accomplish with measurable goals. Dreams are a great start, but the work begins when both specific performance improvement goals and outcome goals have action plans and target dates. Setting daily, monthly and long-term goals build the emotional strength you seek.

Sticking to Commitments: 1 2 3 4 5 6 7 8 9 10

Commitments are obligations that restrict freedom of action. Staying loyal to a written action plan separates the champion from the part-time hobbyist. Hobbyists train when it's convenient. Committed athletes put their sport above their social calendar.

Determination: 1 2 3 4 5 6 7 8 9 10

Determination is the power to persist with a singular fixed purpose. Relentlessly determined to reach your goals. Champions often begin as average athletes with abnormal determination.

Problem-Solving Skills: 1 2 3 4 5 6 7 8 9 10

Identifying the problem is only the first step. Step two is to isolate the causes of the problem. Step three is then to customize the solution to the problem. Creative problem solving requires digging deeper than simply identifying the flaw.

Spotting Patterns and Tendencies: 1 2 3 4 5 6 7 8 9 10

Patterns and tendencies are an individual's predisposition to do something repeatedly. Spotting reoccurring behavior is essential in understanding your strengths and weaknesses as well as defeating a worthy opponent.

Discipline: 1 2 3 4 5 6 7 8 9 10

Discipline is behavior that is judged by how well it follows a set of rules. It is one of the most important emotional elements that turns dreams and goals into accomplishments. It often requires you to choose to train when you'd rather be socializing. Discipline is painful but not nearly as painful as losing to people you should be beating.

Sportsmanship: 1 2 3 4 5 6 7 8 9 10

Sportsmanship is the underlying respect for the game, the rules governing the sport, the opponents and the officials. It's giving it your all and playing with confidence and pride regardless of the outcome.

Focus: 1 2 3 4 5 6 7 8 9 10

Focus is the ability to be single-minded in your interest. Examples include adhering to short-term goals, such as a single play, point or game, all the way towards attaining long-term goals, such as playing a junior Grand Slam or being offered a college athletic scholarship.

Preparation Skills: 1 2 3 4 5 6 7 8 9 10

The life skill of being prepared is especially important in athletics. Preparing properly for battle is one of the most neglected aspects of intermediate athletes. Success stems from total preparation. It is truly the key to preventing a poor performance.

Persistence: 1 2 3 4 5 6 7 8 9 10

Persistence is the continued passion of action in spite of opposition. You need constant energy devoted to your sport. Anything less means that you're a hobbyist. Persistence gets you to the top. Consistency with that persistent frame of mind keeps you there.

Dedication: 1 2 3 4 5 6 7 8 9 10

Dedication is the quality of being committed to a purpose. Dedication to a sport requires passion and commitment to strive for daily improvement. Lazy, non-athletic people use the word "obsessed" to describe the dedicated athletes.

Positive Self-Image: 1 2 3 4 5 6 7 8 9 10

Strong emotional aptitude starts with positive self-esteem. Trusting yourself is a key to competing freely. Changing the negative self-talk into positive internal dialog is a great start.

Revisit your scores above and begin strengthening your emotional aptitude by improving any skill that you graded 7 or less. Keep in mind that solutions are customized to your personality and circumstances. Strong competitive character skills sets stem from life lessons. Achieving spectacular results requires thousands of hours of deliberate customized practice.

Without the foundation of critical "root" skills (optimism, growth mindset and life lessons), a deliberate customized developmental plan will fail to bloom. Subsequently, without proper training; results never materialize.

CONCLUSION

To transform an athlete's match performance, we must first develop their belief systems. By neuro programming their solutions, we prime positive behaviors. Neuro priming is simply a form of optimistic brainwashing.

An analogy I often apply is the similarities between successful athletes and actors. Gifted actors morph into character and memorize their script before arriving on location for the shoot. Aspiring tennis players should do the same. Their character is that of an "athletic warrior." Their script is their pre-set solutions found in this books audio recordings.

Performing at one's peak under stressful match conditions is the goal of every serious tennis competitor. This is why **Neuro Priming for Peak Performance** is an essential addition to an athlete's developmental plan. Great results stem from consistent, correct decision making and great decisions are thought through, organized and pre-planned.

Mental rehearsing increases the athlete's tennis IQ, reprograms old pessimistic beliefs, changes negative behaviors, speeds up the learning process, increase focus duration, assist the athletes in quickly fixing stroke flaws, staying on their script of patterns, as well as coping with stress, nervousness and the fear of failure.

Neuro priming is not only a fundamental component for the professional athlete; it is a necessity for any athlete serious about consistently performing at their potential.

SAMPLE SOLUTIONS

AUDIO #1: Protocols for Stroke Production

For each primary and secondary stroke situation, write a short solution based catchphrase as a customized reminder. Athletes report that by mentally rehearsing their customized stroke solutions they not only fix their technical strokes quicker, they significantly reduce producing the actual errors.

1) Forehands

Drive: Keep my head down.

Short Angle: Hit the outside of the ball.

High & Heavy: Stay planted.

Slice: High to level stroke.

Drop Shot: Decelerate at contact.

Lob: Slow hand swing.

2) Backhands

Drive: Left hand dominant.

Short Angle: Open stance.

High & Heavy: Last step is forward.

Slice: Throw left hand back.

Drop Shot: Light grip pressure.

Lob: Hit higher than the lights.

3) Serves

Flat: Land in the court.

Kick: Toss over the right shoulder.

Slice: Supersize the continental grip.

4) Volleys

Punch: Elbows up.

Transition: Unit turn.

Swing: Plant & swing up.

Drop: Absorb ball speed.

Half: Half groundstroke.

5) Specialty Lobs

Backing Up/ Topspin Lob: Inverted follow through.

Moving Forward/Slice Lob: High finish.

Re-Lob: Volley mechanics.

6) Approach Shot Sequence

Serve and Volley: 1, 2, 3 split.

Chip & Charge: Approach down the line.

Forehand Drive Approach: Into their weakness.

Backhand Drive Approach: Depth.

Backhand Chip Approach: Keep it low with junk.

High and Heavy Delayed Approach: Moonball approach to swing volley.

7) Overheads

Stationary: Two-part swing.

Turn & Run: Cross-over step.

SAMPLE SOLUTIONS

AUDIO #2: Emotional Protocols

Design and list customized solutions for each of the emotional protocols. Athletes who mentally rehearse their pre-set contingency plans (emotional protocols) report cleaner performances and less match time drama consistently.

My Between Point Rituals

External:

1) Go to my towel.
2) Take 3 slow, deep breaths.
3) Look at my strings to relax and control my wondering eyes.

Internal:

1) Get over the last point.
2) Plan the next point's pattern.
3) Relaxation rituals (pre serve-5 bounces)

My Changeover Rituals

External:
Sit down in the shade, get a drink, towel off, and eat if needed.

Internal:
Think: 2 games back (did I hold? Did I break? Why or why not?)

Critical Times to Manage my Adrenaline

1) Towards the end of each game.
2) Towards the end of every set.

My Verbal & Physical Triggers to Combat Choking

Verbal:
Let's go, Get on script, Focus, One point at a time.

Physical:
Swoosh, shadow swings, move your feet, Pump up the energy.

My Verbal & Physical Triggers for Panicking

Verbal:
Calm down, relax, stay on script, and breathe slow.

Physical:
Take more time, go to the towel, re-tie ponytail or shoelaces, take a bathroom break.

Energy Flow Management *(Check Box If Understood.)*

☐ I'll control the playing speed of the match.

☐ I'll control the positive energy of the match.

☐ I'll inflate my fight to deflate their will to battle.

Game Day/Pre-Match Preparation
(Check Box If Understood)

- ☐ I will listen to my audio tapes to pre-set an excellent performance.

- ☐ I will morph into an athletic warrior by: *Getting into character and staying on script.*

- ☐ I will warm up my primary & secondary strokes.

- ☐ I will go for a short run right before the match.

- ☐ I will focus on performing excellently ... not perfect.

- ☐ I will trust my training and my awesomeness.

Weekly Training Reminders *(Check Box If Understood)*

- ☐ I will record and watch my actual matches with a high IQ coach.

- ☐ I will focus my training on serving and returning serve.

- ☐ I will rehearse my top seven patterns weekly.

- ☐ I will pay attention to the cause of my errors.

- ☐ I will abide by The Laws of Offense Neutral and Defensive in my shots selections.

Letting Go of Perfectionism *(Check Box If Understood)*

- ☐ I'll shoot for excellence, not perfection.

- ☐ I'll try to win 66% of the points.

- ☐ I'll relax and give 80% versus 110% effort.

- ☐ I'll eliminate energy-wasting antics.

SAMPLE SOLUTIONS

AUDIO #3: Mental Protocols (SINGLES) Essentials

Design and list your customized strategic approach to the game of singles. Mentally rehearsing your solutions to the wide range of mental skills is essential in high-performance tennis. Athletes report that by customizing their mental solutions they perform on script more consistently and efficiently.

My "A" Game Plan Is: Hard hitting baseliners.

My "B" Game Plan Is: Steady, counter puncher, retriever.

My Shot Tolerance Level Is: 5 balls

My Primary Top Seven Patterns

1) Most Proficient Pattern Serving to the Deuce Side:
   Slice serve to the T (their backhand) then inside-out forehand into their backhand.

2) Most Proficient Pattern Serving to the Advantage Side:
   Kick serve wide (to the backhand) then crosscourt forehand.

3) Most Proficient Return of Serve Position and Type of Return Versus a Big First Serve:
Deuce: Stand 5 ft. behind the baseline. Match the ball speed and aim deep down the middle.
Ad: Stand 5 ft. behind the baseline. Match the ball speed and aim crosscourt to their backhand.

4) Most Proficient Return of Serve Position and Type of Return Versus a Weak or Second Serve:
Deuce: Position 3 steps inside the baseline, hit down the line into their weaker backhand.
Ad: Position 3 steps inside the baseline, hit crosscourt into their weaker backhand.

5) Most Proficient Rally Pattern to Get Opponents Vulnerable:
Roll my short angles to get them moving. Then hit to the opening or behind the runner.

6) Most Proficient Short Ball Option:
Crush short balls down the line.

7) Most Proficient Net Rushing Patterns:
Moonball approach to swing volley.

I Will Profile My Opponent's Game By
(Check Box If Understood)

- ☐ Recognize their "style" of play.
- ☐ Spot their favorite "top seven patterns" and shutting them down.
- ☐ Identify their "frustration tolerance" level.
- ☐ Determine their stroke and movement strengths and weaknesses.
- ☐ Recognize their "shot tolerance."

Score Management

Positive game points require:

Aggressive positioning and offensive play.

Negative game points require:

Neutralizing position and applying more margins.

Zonal Tennis

Court Zone Percentages:

I hit the shot the zone demands. If the ball lands short, I attack. If the ball lands mid-court- I apply building shots. If the ball lands deep- I hit high and heavy.

Air Zone Percentages:

When I'm inside the court- I aim 2-3 ft. above the net.
When I'm around the baseline- I aim 4-5 ft. above the net.
When I'm behind the court- I aim 8 ft. above the net.

Broad Vision/Anticipatory Clues

When the ball is leaving my racket and is traveling towards their side, I look at the big picture. I spot the court zone it is landing in and the opponent's court position and their strike zone.

Margins

I'll apply Safe Margins by:

Aiming 3 feet above the net and 3 feet inside the lines.

Controlling the Baseline

1) I'll choose to hit forehands 70 % of the time.

2) I'll choose to hit backhands 30 % of the time.

Approaching the Net Wisely

1) I'll divide the width of the court into two zones.

2) I'll hit short balls landing in 75% of the court to their backhand and 25% to their forehand.

Two Tactical Changes to Consider When I'm Losing:

1) Raising my level - hit harder, closer to the lines and attack successfully.

2) Sabotage their level - moonball, drop, slice, or junk ball.

Self-Destruction Solutions *(Check Box If Understood)*

1) If I'm losing to a "toad," I'll:

   ☐ Simply hit 3 balls down the center.
   ☐ Apply the "bounce-hit" method.
   ☐ Return to my script.
   ☐ Focus on simply winning 3 points in a row.

2) If my game isn't working and I'm losing to a retriever, I will pull them out of their comfort zone by:

   A) Applying my short angle "side door" building shots and patterns.

   B) Applying my moonball approach to swing volley or drop volley pattern.

   C) I'll hit drop shots, bring the opponent into the net and then pass or lob.

3) If my game isn't working and I'm losing to a hard hitting baseliner, I will pull them out of their comfort zone by:

A) Mixing the spin speed and trajectory of my shots- giving them no rhythm.

B) I'll focus on getting 75% first serves in. Especially to their backhand. (I don't want to give them any 2nd serves to crush.)

C) I'll focus on more depth. Applying my high & heavy ground strokes pushes them back and keeping the ball out of the primary strike zone.

When to Choose Building Shots Versus Winners
(Check Box If Understood.)

- ☐ Returning a first serve.
- ☐ Rallying a deep ball.
- ☐ On a negative mega point.

SAMPLE SOLUTIONS

AUDIO #4: Mental Protocols (DOUBLES) Essentials

Design and list your customized approach to the game of doubles by mentally rehearsing strategic solutions to the wide range of mental skills needed in high-performance tennis. Athletes report that by applying mental rehearsals, they prime the pumps and consistently perform better in competition.

Choosing the Right Partner

A) Pick someone better than you. Name a few candidates:
Mickey, Steven, and Matt

B) The hammer & wedge partnership. Name a few candidates:
Matt, Sam, and Mark

Warm Up For Doubles Matches with Doubles Skills Sets Not Singles (*Practice in the manner you're expected to perform*)

List 5 Warm-Up Doubles Strategies:
1) Mini tennis and baseline rally crosscourt only with alleys versus rallying down the middle.
2) Serving from the doubles serve position and the various return of serves specifics for doubles.
3) Volleying/Overhead versus dippers/lobs.
4) Approach shot sequences from both deuce and ad.
5) Volley war- quick hands.

Choosing Sides, Deuce or Advantage, Points to Consider *(Check Box If Understood.)*

☐ Stroke strengths & weaknesses

☐ Emotional strengths & weaknesses

Partnership Communication

A) De-Stressing Topics (List 2)
1. Share optimistic observations.
2. Share a proactive attitude.

B) Opponent Profiling (List 2)
1. Discuss their stroke, movement and positioning strengths and weaknesses.
2. Talk about their shifting formations, their frustration tolerance and their pattern play.

C) Tactical Options (List 2)
1 Consider our own stroke, positioning, strength and weaknesses. Design strategies to expose our strengths and hide our weaknesses.
2 Review the score, managing positive and negative big points and how to approach them differently.

D) Facial Expressions, Body Language & Tone of Voice Matters (List 2)
1. Pumping up my partner with smiles, fist pumps, moving feet, and shadow swinging to show them I'm in it to win it!

2. Say, Let's go! Right now! To keep my partner focused on this singular point- avoiding outcome thoughts.

E) Hand Signals Yes or No (List Signal)

First serve placement (poach or stay)...Second serve placement (poach or stay.)

Choose Your Best & 2nd Best Doubles System
(When & Why):

A) One Up and One Back

    When:
    1. Serving 2nd serves.
    2. Returning big 1st serves.

    Why:
    To progress from a defensive situation to a neutral situation then into an offensive court position.

B) Both Rush the Net

    When:
    1. Serving 1st serve.
    2. Returning weak 2nd serves.

    Why:
    Apply pressure, take away their recovery and reaction time, and to increase winning angles.

C) Double Back

When:
1. Return a big 1st serve.
2. Serving a weak 2nd serve.

Why:
To take away the opponent's net positioning target. If we are both back, we can expose our killer groundstrokes and hide our fragile volleys.

D) "I" Formation

When:
Serving to an opponent who is crushing their cross court returns.

Why:
To shut down their successful returns and make them beat us with their secondary plans.

The Role of Each Position in Doubles

1) Server:
Get 75% of 1st serves in. Serve to the opponent's backhand.

2) Server's Partner:
Follow the serve, stay on wide balls, poach on T serves.

3) Returner:
Plan A- Crosscourt drive. Plan B- Crosscourt chip. Plan C- Lob the net player.

4) Returner's Partner:
Call the serve. Move up or back 2 big steps depending on the quality of my partner's return.

Doubles Reminders *(Check Box If Understood)*

☐ Hit Long to long, short to short.

☐ Angles creates angles.

☐ Abide by the laws of offense, neutral and defense.

☐ High volleys are power volleys and low volleys are drop volleys.

☐ Net players have priority for any ball.

☐ When in doubt "Down the middle, solves the riddle."

☐ 70% of the points last 0-4 strikes, 20% last 5-9 and 10% go 10 & over.

☐ 78% of their winners come from their forehand and 22% from their backhand.

☐ Move together -synchronized with an imaginary 10 ft. rope.

☐ Guard the center. (Only worry about your alley if your partner hits wide into the opposing doubles alley)

When to Poach: *(Check Box If Understood)*

    ☐ Partner serves to the backhand.
    ☐ Return of serve partner hits at the feet of the rushing server.
    ☐ Opponent is hitting inside strokes.
    ☐ Partner has hit High and Heavy & opponent is falling backward.

When to Choose a Building Shot Versus Going for A Risky Winner: *(Check Box If Understood)*

    ☐ Returning a solid first serve.

    ☐ Rallying a deep groundstroke.

    ☐ On a negative game point.

Why Doubles is a Blast: *(Check Box If Understood)*

    ☐ Less stressful because I'm sharing the fight.

    ☐ Teamwork in solving the physical, mental & emotional puzzles.

    ☐ My secondary strokes will improve.

    ☐ My problem-solving skills will improve.

    ☐ I'll get a great workout —warm-up for singles.

SAMPLE SOLUTIONS

AUDIO #5: Essential Life Skills Development

Upon the completion of the life skills assessment, any life skill graded a 7 or lower needs improvement. Google or YouTube the life skill then draft a paragraph describing your customized developmental plan to improve the skill.

1) **Time Management**

   Pick up a daily/weekly planner at staples. Each week plug in my customized components including off court gym, off court cardio, primary and secondary stroke development, pattern repetition, mental rehearsals, match video analysis and sets/live balls.

2) **Discipline**

   Off-Court- I'll get up early and do my off-court training before school or work. Practice sessions- I'll practice in the manner I'm expected to perform. Match play- I'll choose to stay on scrip and to focus remaining in the present versus future thoughts.

3) **Handling Adversity**

   I'll add negative scoring to every drill session to keep me accountable for unforced errors. It'll help me with my perseverance and resiliency as well. I'll also focus on the solution versus the problem. Being solution orientated is an optimistic, positive approach.

ABOUT THE AUTHOR

Frank Giampaolo is an award-winning coach, popular international speaker, and sports researcher. He is an instructional writer for ITF (International Tennis Federation) Coaching & Sports Science Review, UK Tennis magazine, the USPTA, Tennis Magazine and Tennis View Magazine. Frank is both a USPTA and PTR educator, a Tennis Congress Factuality Member, and has been a featured speaker at the Australian Grand Slam Coaches Convention, the PTR GB Wimbledon Conference, and Wingate Sports Institute (Israel.)

Frank is the bestselling author of Championship Tennis (Human Kinetics Publishing), Raising Athletic Royalty, The Tennis Parent's Bible (volume I & II), Emotional Aptitude In Sports, and The Mental Emotional Workbook Series (How to Attract a College Scholarship, International Player Evaluation, Match Chart Collection, Match Day Preparation and Blunders and Cures). His television appearances include The NBC Today Show, OCN-World Team Tennis, Fox Sports, Tennis Canada and Tennis Australia.

Frank founded The Tennis Parents Workshops in 1998, conducting workshops across the United States, Mexico, Israel, New Zealand, Australia, England, Canada and Spain. Frank's commitment to coaching excellence helped develop approximately 100 National Champions, hundreds of NCAA athletes, numerous NCAA All-Americans and several professional athletes. His innovative approach has made him a worldwide leader in athletic-parental education. Frank is currently the Vice Chair of the USTA/SCTA Coaches Commission.

Frank Giampaolo Workshops

Bring Frank and The Mental/Emotional Workshops to your town: Parent Workshops, Mental/Emotional Workshops, One-on-One Private Sessions, High School Workshops, College Team Workshops, Camps, Groups and Academy Workshops.

Contact Information

Email: FGSA@earthlink.net
Website: www.MaximizingTennisPotential.com
Facebook:
http://facebook.com/FrankGiampaoloBooks.The Tennis Parent Bible

69712139R00047

Made in the USA
San Bernardino, CA
20 February 2018